KU-363-067

BLACK COUNTRY

BLACK COUNTRY

Liz Berry

Chatto & Windus
LONDON

Published by Chatto & Windus

6 8 10 9 7

Copyright © Liz Berry 2014

Liz Berry has asserted her right under the Copyright, Designs
and Patents Act 1988 to be identified as the author of this work

This book is sold subject to the condition that it shall not,
by way of trade or otherwise, be lent, resold, hired out,
or otherwise circulated without the publisher's prior
consent in any form of binding or cover other than that
in which it is published and without a similar condition,
including this condition, being imposed
on the subsequent purchaser

First published in Great Britain by
Chatto & Windus
Random House, 20 Vauxhall Bridge Road,
London SW1V 2SA
www.randomhouse.co.uk

Addresses for companies within The Random House Group Limited can be found at:
www.randomhouse.co.uk/offices.htm

The Random House Group Limited Reg. No. 954009

A CIP catalogue record for this book
is available from the British Library

ISBN 9780701188573

The Random House Group Limited supports the Forest Stewardship Council® (FSC®),
the leading international forest-certification organisation. Our books carrying the
FSC label are printed on FSC®-certified paper. FSC is the only forest-certification
scheme supported by the leading environmental organisations, including Greenpeace.
Our paper procurement policy can be found at www.randomhouse.co.uk/environment

Typeset by Palimpsest Book Production Limited, Falkirk, Stirlingshire
Printed in Great Britain by Clays Ltd, St Ives plc

For my family, with love

Contents

BLACK COUNTRY

Bird

When I became a bird, Lord, nothing could not stop me.

The air feathered
                    as I knelt
by my open window for the charm –
                    black on gold,
                    last star of the dawn.

Singing, they came:
                    throstles, jenny wrens,
jack squalors swinging their anchors through the clouds.

My heart beat like a wing.

I shed my nightdress to the drowning arms of the dark,
my shoes to the sun's widening mouth.

Bared,
   I found my bones hollowing to slender pipes,
      my shoulder blades tufting down.
      I   spread   my flight-greedy arms
to watch my fingers jewelling like ten hummingbirds,
my feet callousing to knuckly claws.
      As my lips calcified to a hooked kiss

silence

      then an exultation of larks filled the clouds
and, in my mother's voice, chorused:
   Tek flight, chick, goo far fer the winter.

So I left girlhood behind me like a blue egg

                                and stepped off
               from the window ledge.

How light I was

as they lifted me up from Wren's Nest
bore me over the edgelands of concrete and coal.

I saw my grandmother waving up from her fode,
               looped
    the infant school and factory,
               let the zephrs carry me   out to the coast.

Lunars I flew

               battered and tuneless

    the storms turned me inside out like a fury,
there wasn't one small part of my body didn't bawl.

Until I felt it at last   the rush of squall thrilling my wing
             and I knew my voice
was no longer words but song   black upon black.

I raised my throat to the wind
                and this is what I sang…

charm birdsong or dawn chorus; *jack squalor* swallow; *fode* yard

Birmingham Roller

'We spent our lives down in the blackness ... those birds
brought us up to the light'
    – JIM SHOWELL, *Tumbling Pigeons and the Black Country*

Wench, yowm the colour of ower town:
concrete, steel, oily rainbow of the cut.

Ower streets am in yer wings,
ower factory chimdeys plumes on yer chest,

yer heart's the china ower owd girls dust
in their tranklement cabinets.

Bred to dazzlin in backyards by men
whose onds grew soft as feathers

just to touch you, cradle you from egg
through each jeth-defying tumble.

Little acrobat of the terraces,
we'm winged when we gaze at you

jimmucking the breeze, somersaulting through
the white-breathed prayer of January

and rolling back up like a babby's yo-yo
caught by the open donny of the clouds.

cut canal; *tranklement* bits and bobs, ornaments; *onds* hands;
jeth death; *jimmucking* shaking; *donny* hand, especially a child's

Homing

For years you kept your accent
in a box beneath the bed,
the lock rusted shut by hours of elocution
how now brown cow
the teacher's ruler across your legs.

We heard it escape sometimes,
a guttural *uh* on the phone to your sister,
saft or *blart* to a taxi driver
unpacking your bags from his boot.
I loved its thick drawl, *g*'s that rang.

Clearing your house, the only thing
I wanted was that box, jemmied open
to let years of lost words spill out –
bibble, fittle, tay, wum,
vowels ferrous as nails, consonants

you could lick the coal from.
I wanted to swallow them all: the pits,
railways, factories thunking and clanging
the night shift, the red brick
back-to-back you were born in.

I wanted to forge your voice
in my mouth, a blacksmith's furnace;
shout it from the roofs,
send your words, like pigeons,
fluttering for home.

Bostin Fittle

At Nanny's I ate brains for tea,
mashed with hard-boiled egg,
or trotters, groaty pudding,
faggots minced with kidney and suet.

Right bostin fittle, Nanny said.
She knew hunger, knew how
to press a blade sure and firm
on the pig's fat ribs, clack the neck

of the cockerel. An apprentice,
I studied her careful craft:
the sweet heart hidden in the rotten
cabbage, chitterlings plaited

like a rope of hair.
Elbow deep in rabbit, floury
chunks of lard, I touched
my lips to the hide of the past:

salty, dark, unexpected
as the rook she'd baked
for her bride-feast, that flew
crawing from her hands to his tongue.

bostin fittle great food

Black Country

Commuters saw it first, vast
on the hillside by the A41,
a wingless Pegasus, hooves
kicking road into the distance.

It had appeared over night.
A black shadow on the scrub,
galloping above the gates
of the derelict factories,

facing East, towards the pits,
mouth parted as if it would
swallow the sun that rose
from behind the winding gear.

Word spread. Crowds gathered.
Kids, someone said,
but when they examined its flanks
they found pure coal,

coal where none had been mined
in years, where houses
still collapsed into empty shafts
and hills bore scars.

A gift from the underworld,
hauling the past
from the dead earth. Old men
knelt to breathe the smoke

of its mane, whisper
in its ear, walked away
in silence, fists clenched,
faces streaked with tears.

Nailmaking

Nailing was wenches' werk.
Give a girl of eight an anvil and a little ommer
and by God er'd swing it,
batter the glowing iron into tidy spikes
ready fer hoofing some great sod oss
who'd lost its shoe in the muck.

The nimble ones was best,
grew sharp and quick as the nails they struck
from the scorching fire.
Eighteen, er could turn out two hundred an hour,
tongue skimming the soot on er lips,
onds moulding heat.

In the small brick nailshop
four of 'em werked wi' faces glistening
in the hot smoke. Fust the point was forged
then the rod sunk deep into the bore
so the head could be punched –
round fer regulars, diamond fer frost nails.

*Marry a nailing fella and yo'll be a pit oss
fer life,* er sisters had told er,
but er'd gone to him anyway in er last white frock
and found a new black ommer
waiting fer er in 'is nailshop
under a tablecloth veil.

ommer hammer;   *er* her, she;   *oss* horse

The Red Shoes

Crimson. Like flames, like the first sear of blood
that came in the night and daubed a heart on my bedsheets.
They made blushes look pale.

On Saturdays, I pressed my lips to the steamy glass
of the shoe-shop window and blew them
a kiss. I was mad for their patent,

rubies that glistened up a dress,
flushed thighs with fever.
I was tired of childhood, black and navy.

I smashed the belly of the fat piggy bank
and stole ten pounds from my mother's purse,
waltzed to school in them, legs cocky

as girls in the science block lifted their eyes
from pipettes and streamed from the lab
to watch me dance. Some girls clapped.

Miss Wetherby rang my mother
to take me home. But I skipped through the playground,
out of the gates that led to the terraces,

the parcels of garden where rickety sheds
burst into flames as my shoes grazed them.
By the factory, I danced a rumba,

drew lads whistling from the high windows,
catcalling my name into the rosy smoke.
I tore my school skirt, threw my tie in the gutter,

felt my voice hatching in my throat
as I danced through the waste ground
to the filthy canal. There the sky darkened.

The hedges became copses, fierce with nettles.
In the branches, a single glove hung from the brambles.
The dance grew wild, a tarantella

through the forest's darkness, the steps flowing
like a thick pulse of blood.
I heard the screams of girls who had danced

before me, their ankles severed, toes
still tapping, white as wounded doves.
But I was not their kind. I out-danced the axe,

the silent woodcutter, the traps waiting with rusty jaws.
I danced so fast my shoes scorched the air
and the sun laid the sky down, crimson, at my feet.

Tipton-On-Cut

Come wi' me, bab, wum to Tipton-on-Cut,
the real Little Venice, reisty and wild as the midden in August.
We'll glide along Telford's fabled waterways
on board *Summat in the Waerter* or *Our Wench of Brum*.
Or like Lady Godiva, we'll trot in on an oss
who's guttling clover at the edge of the bonk.
We'll goo straight to the sweet cabbage heart of 'local':
shout 'oiright' to blokes lugging spuds in their allotments,
yawning in the dark to call centres and factories;
we'll flirt wi' Romeos, grooming at *Tip'N'Cut*,
sunning emselves to creosote fences down the tan shop.
We'll blow a kiss to ower bostin native wenches:
owd uns, young uns, all dolled-up,
white as bingo-china or brown as the cut,
some wi' their babbies and some wi' their bargains,
some salwaar'd in blue-pop and cherryade silk.
Come, let's raise a toast to Aynuk in *The Fountain*
or *Noah's Ark* wi' its pairs of china dogs and brass osses.
We'll ate faggits and pays, batters, baltis,
crack ower molars on *Sanjay's Black Country Scratchings*
then goo three rounds, bare-knuckle, in the Jubilee Park
wi' a lad the spit of the Tipton Slasher,
whipping off 'is trackie top in the randan,
wet wi' sweat the flavour of Banks's.
If we win, we'll give thanks at the Holy Fires Baptist,
the hallowed ground of the Tipton Ladies,
the mosque all gemmed up gold and fairylit,
pay ower respects, wi' the owd boys,
at the crumbling altar of the BDF Steelworks.
Love, we'll gather the finest gifts of the region:

an anchor, a cow pie, a tumbling pigeon,
that metal oss that prances by the railway crossing,
a wammel in every hue under the sun!
Then we'll nightowl away in knees-up splendour:
kaylighed, singing *Oh Tiptonia*
as we lie on ower baltied bellies on the towpath
to sup the moon, like the head of a pint,
from ower cut.

wum home;   *cut* canal;   *oss* horse;   *guttling* chewing;   *bonk* bank;
Aynuk Enoch, traditional Black Country comedy character;
pays grey peas;   *Tipton Slasher* famous Tipton bareknuckle boxer;
Banks's Banks's Bitter;   *randan* fight;   *wammel* dog, especially a mongrel;
kaylighed drunk

The Patron Saint of School Girls

Agnes had her lamb and her black curls,
Bernadette, her nun's frock,
but I was just a school girl,
glimpsed the holy spirit in the blue flare
of a Bunsen burner, saw a skeleton
weep in a biology lesson.

My miracles were revelations.
I saved seventeen girls from a fire that rose
like a serpent behind the bike sheds,
cured the scoliosis of a teacher
who hadn't lifted her head to sing a hymn
in years. I fed the dinner hall
on one small cake and a carton of milk.

A cult developed. The Head Girl
kissed my cheek in the dark-room,
first years wrote my name
on the flyleaf of their hymn books,
letters appeared in my school bag,
a bracelet woven from a blonde plait.

My faith grew strong.
At night I lay awake hearing prayers
from girls as far as Leeds and Oxford,
comprehensives in Nottingham.
I granted supplications for A-levels,
pleas for the cooling of unrequited love,
led a sixth form in Glasgow to unforeseen triumph
in the hockey cup final.

Love flowed out of me like honey
from a hive, I was sweet with holiness,
riding home on the school bus
imparting my blessings.
I was ready for wings,
to be lifted upwards like sun streaming
through the top deck windows;
to wave goodbye to school and disappear
in an astonishing ring of brightness.

5th Dudley Girl Guides

Your plain faces are lovely as bunting
in the sunlight while you pitch your tents

calling each other to pull guy-ropes taut
crawling easy as lads   lifting

the silver pole inside the green canvas.
I would like to be you again, just for a moment,

catching another wench's smile like a frisbee
raising your flag in the expectant air.

When I Was a Boy

I was a boy every weekday afternoon
the year I was seven –
hitched my school skirt into shorts,
flattened my hair with a black ballet band,
wore my brother's elasticated tie.

I had many different names:
sometimes *Paul* or *Steven* (boy next door),
sometimes *Dean* (rough)
or *Jean Paul* (exotic), here on exchange.
I didn't bother with chit-chat, got straight

down to the real stuff: an aeroplane
made from homework that gave papercuts
as it flew, thin sugary sticks I sucked
like cigarettes then tossed out the window,
the stubble I was cultivating.

I built remarkable things: a model
of our school with working windows,
a ukulele. I twirled two potato guns
on my cocked thumbs. The girls loved me:
held my hand whilst I ignored them,

swaggered down the street, ripe
for danger or rode my bike
with my blouse off, admiring my reflection
in wing mirrors, legs kicked
in a triumphant V, fist in the air.

Trucker's Mate

The A1 is the loneliest. Four hundred
and nine miles down the spine of the country,
only the firefly of a fag tip to keep you steady.
A man needs some company,
an eye on the map, a hand on the radio.
Ten four, hammer down, breaker breaker.

He made a man of me, rubbed me
smooth with engine grease, taught me how
to pull a flatbed, take an unsigned route,
draw the curtains against the prying eyes
of headlights. As other lorries trundle home,
we push onwards, the road a romance.

I was a kid that first night. Birmingham
to Folkestone. The junctions looping
and racing above us, his hand on my leg.
In the woods beside the layby, I pressed my tongue
into the sap of a pine tree as I pissed,
already half in love with him.

Now belly to back in the cab, his vertebrae
like cat's eyes guiding me down,
I think of the M6 Toll, lined with two million
pulped Mills and Boons; how love is buried
in unlooked for places, kept secret as us.
In the darkness his breath hums like an engine.

The First Path

When you found me there was nothing beautiful about me.
I wasn't even human
                            just a mongrel
kicked out into the snow on Maundy Thursday
when all the world was sorrow,
when old girls' hands were raw as they cracked
the ice on their birdbaths,
when the priest wept in Saint Jude the Apostle
as he knelt to wash the feet of an altar boy.

I was filth,
              running away from God-knows-what,
my haunches sore with bruises,
my spine knuckling the ruin of my coat.

Running through the town
                            away from the horses
who bowed their heads to the donkey-bite,
away from the boy in the bus shelter
                                    who turned from me
to receive a snowflake
like a wafer on his tongue.

Lord help me
              I did things I would once
have been ashamed of.

Now no one would come near me,
                            they feared

the hunger that gnawed and whined in my bones,
the hurt I would carry into their houses.

Only you dared follow
                        upon the track
of my bloodied paw prints in the ice,
where the trees held snow in their arms
like winding sheets.
                        You came for me there
                                    close, low,
calling a name that was not mine.
Calling *wench, my wench*
as the tongues of the church bells rang mute.

At your scent on the air,
                        I shot
through the woods – a grey cry –
so raw only the dusk could touch me

but you were patient,
                        waited
through the dense muffled hours
until darkness dropped and I sank into the midden
behind the factory
and the chimneys cast a wreath of ash upon me.

            You touched me then,
         when I was nothing but dirt,
took off your glove and laid your palm upon my throat,
slipped the loop of the rope,

                    lifted me
into your arms and carried me home
                              along the first path.

In the banks the foxes barked *alleluia alleluia.*

The blizzard tumbled upon us like confetti
and I, little bitch, blue bruise,
saw myself in your eyes:
                         a bride.

donkey-bite small patch of wasteland or grazing ground

Taps

Death came for me in Maytime,
through the poplars, where I'd pitched the small tent
of my body and lain down inside it
all my white bones surrendering
as in those dawns at Girl Guide camp
when I woke pressed like a bookmark
between the opening pages of other young women.
And when I lay still, I heard it.
Come Wrens and Robins, sweet Blackbirds
with your hair newly feathered,
come Kingfishers with your burnt sienna neckers
and teal blouses, come flitting
through the beeches, embroidering the woods
with your voices;
come with your arms full of ferns,
come with kindling and moss
and a pair of silver saucepans clinking Taps;
come still-dreaming girls from your canvas nests.
Come now, for the sun lifts the veil of night.
Quickly, girls, come.

The Year We Married Birds

That year, with men turning thirty
still refusing to fly the nest,
we married birds instead.

Migrating snow buntings
swept into offices in the city,
took flocks of girls for Highland weddings.

Magpies smashed jewellers' windows,
kites hovered above bridal shops,
a pigeon in Trafalgar Square learnt to kneel.

Sales of nesting boxes soared.
Soon cinemas were wild as woods in May
while restaurants served worms.

By June, a Russian kittiwake wed
the Minister's daughter, gave her two
freckled eggs, a mansion on a cliff.

My own groom was a kingfisher:
enigmatic, bright. He gleamed in a metallic
turquoise suit, taught me about fishing

in the murky canal. We honeymooned
near the Wash, the saltmarshes
booming with courting bittern.

When I think of that year, I remember best
the fanning of his feathers
on my cheek, his white throat,

how every building, every street rang
with birdsong. How girls' wedding dresses
lifted them into the trees like wings.

The Silver Birch

Let me tell you about the sex I knew
                              before sex

in the beginning   when I was a creature
when I took the bit of your hair
    between my teeth
and pushed your face to the silver birch
while you whimpered
                at the fur of me

how I came alive in dens and copses
          in the tall grass
where the sky lurched violet

yes those days

when I was neither girl or boy
but my body was a sheaf
                        of unwritten-upon paper
          now folding unfolding
              origaming new

days   pale as the silver birch

when sex was a pebble thrown
                        into the pond of me
                                        rippling out
when I held your fingers in my mouth
as the woods hummed electric with sensation
now   they sang   now

and everything was sex then

                        although I could not name it
it was the scar upon your shoulder
                an arrow of light through the beeches

days   days wet as cuckoo spit

when I lay skin-bare in the field
each insect   jack-in-the-hedge
every bowing poppy touching me

      oh my body was a meadow then
    and you could lie in me forever
               and still not be done

Sow

'Dainty footwear turns a young lady into an altogether
more beautiful creature...'

– ELIZA SELL, Etiquette for Ladies

Trottering down the oss road in me new hooves
I'm farmyardy sweet, fresh from the filth
of straw an' swill, the trembly-leg sniff
of the slaughter wagon. A guzzler, gilt.
Trollopy an' canting. Root yer tongue beneath
me frock an' gulp the brute stench of the sty.

I've stopped denying meself: nibbling
grateful as a pet on baby-leaves, afeared
of the glutton of belly an' rump. I've sunk
an' when lads howd out opples on soft city palms
I guttle an' spit, fer I need a mon
wi' a body like a trough of tumbly slop
to bury me snout in.

All them saft years of hiding at 'ome
then prancing like a pony fer some sod to bridle
an' shove down the pit, shying away
from 'is dirty fists. All them nights,
me eyes rolling white in the dark when the sow I am
was squailin an' biting to gerrout.

Now no mon dare scupper me,
nor fancy-arse bints, fer I've kicked the fence
an' I'm riling on me back in the muck,
out of me mind wi' grunting pleasure,

trotters pointing to the heavens like chimdey pots,
sticking V to the cockerel
prissy an' crowing on 'is high church spire.

oss road street;   *gilt* sow;   *canting* cheeky or saucy;   *guttle* chew;
mon man;   s*aft* foolish;   *squalin* squealing or crying

Carmella

Oh Carmella,
Our Lady of the Hairdressers,
yours are the wenches:
the blondes and the redheads,
the mothers getting permed reading *Take a Break,*
the little junior frizzling her cowlick in the mirror.
Yours is the halo of the hairspray
and the lovely silver can-can dancing scissors.

Let your hands make light
work of us,
our heads tipped back
in your small basin, our skulls
and all their tranklements in your palms.
Baptise us, chick, with council pop
and shampoo kaylighing as sweet cider.

Spoon our dripping heads
beneath your breasts,
your red-sequined heart thumpity thump
inside your blouse, your fingers moving
like beams of sun through cloud,
and whisper the parable of the wench,
who modelled once at a motorbike show
and made men in leather fall
to their knees.

As we shut our eyes, remind us
that beneath these trackies, this hair,
we're ecstatic creatures,

capable still of being lifted from our bodies.
Up we go   up
from your queendom of wenches
until our heads are in the starry sky
and far below us
on earth, the driers sigh and hmmmn
in their orbit.

council pop tap water;   *kaylighing* intoxicating

Owl

My body wakes with the constellations,
star-by-star in the stifling darkness. I glide
over the dog-guarded houses, the cattle

lowing in the moonlit kraal. A parcel
of skin, teeth, bones falls,
a skeletal warning. I come with messages

from the darkest place. An infant coughing blood
in the village, a woman on the bed of the Ruhuhu river,
her eye-sockets hollow, a fist printing a boy's face.

I trouble the shadows with my mourning song:
hoot-hoo-hoo-buhuhu-hoo. They shot my love
with a wooden arrow and nailed his white chest

to the doorframe to drive me away.
I drew closer. Shape-shifters conjured my body
and I welcomed their wickedness. I bore them

into the dreaming houses, the beds of lovers,
mothers nursing slumbering babies. I carried curses
between my claws, drought in my beak.

A fury, I plunged through the sultry blackness,
over children with bows, to seek my love,
his pitiful heart face, the shape of sorrow.

The Black Delph Bride

I was the cut
lovered atween the groanin locks,
a nail on the anvil
waitin to be punched,
a wench unbucklin the collar of a bear
an' dancin into 'is paws to waltz.
Down at Black Delph
I was, I was...

Black Delph, Black Delph, my girl she floats,
her bridesmaids: eels and voles and stoats.

Snuff your lantern
Hear her sing

I was the tune
foxes yelped in the nettled banks,
a bonnet torn off
an' trampled in the danks,
a minnow, hooked tight, an' riling
in 'is grasp.
Down at Black Delph
I was, I was...

Black Delph, Black Delph, my girl she sinks,
her wedding gown: fishing net, weeds and mink.

Jedden your engine
Hear her sing

I was a Wet-the-Bed laid on the tongue,
a Sorrow-In-Winter, a muckled thorn,
a coiled rope
waitin to be hung,
the black oss that stumbles
like a dream from the fog, unbridled, unshod.
Down at Black Delph
I was, I was.

Down at Black Delph I was.

cut canal;   *jedden* deaden;   *oss* horse

32

The Bone Orchard Wench

Haunted er was, allus looking for Jeth.
Er'd try and catch 'Im in the cataracty eyes
of the owd girls, taste 'Im on the coins they gid er.
Ear to the marble, er'd listen for 'Im, gulp the air
when the crem chimdey sighed.
Spying on a burial in the snow, er caught 'Is face
in the winder of slow-rolling hearse,
smoke ghouling from the wreath of 'Is mouth.

Er gid up gooin home, night-owled,
robbed a bear from a babby's grave, unpicked its stuffing
so woodlice scrawled tissiky on er onds.
Er felt that bone orchard stare allus gawping through er
til er lay, scrattin in the soil of a plot,
the silver body of a spade in er arms.

bone orchard cemetery; *jeth* death; *gid* gave

Gosty Hill

Out of the cut at Gosty Hill,
I fished a marble-stoppered bottle.

Opened, it sang…

Come to me by *Iris, Rose of Sharon,*
by *Speedwell, Teasel, Ragwort, Yarrow*
by *Jenny Wren, Dove, Jack Squalor, Throstle,*
I'll be waitin at Delph Run with brick in me ond.

Ocker Hill, Engine Arm, Withymoor Pit
I baptised mah wench in the dark o' the cut

Come to me by *Vixen, Mole, Adder*
by *Perseverence, Euphrates, Hero, Endeavor*
by *Pearl, Opal, Garnet, Silver*
I'll be waitin at Wren's Nest with rope in me ond.

Ocker Hill, Engine Arm, Withymoor Pit
I baptised mah wench in the dark o' the cut

Come to me by *Severn, Avon, Ouse*
by *Shrophire Lass, Gel, Sweetheart, Wench*
by *Ezekiah, Elijah, Azriel, Zeus,*
I'll be waitin at Tat Bank with iron in me ond.

Ocker Hill, Engine Arm, Withymoor Pit
I baptised mah wench in the dark o' the cut

Come in the dusk with a snuffed-out lamp,
yer bonnet a veil, yer petticoat damp,
leave yer boat oss kissin his teeth to the bank
I'll be waitin at Shutend with steel in me ond.

cut canal; *ond* hand; *oss* horse

The Last Lady Ratcatcher

I was the last Lady Ratcatcher.
Bore the scar o' two yellow incisors
on mah wedding finger.

Each night I crept out, cage ready,
mah mind eager as a trap
on a neck bone

mah beauty legendary
in a cape o' brown fur, a belt o' silver rats
scrawling from buckle to back.

I wheeled the black rats
in a squirming tea-chest
round the dog pits of Bilston

brought the pretty ones wum,
kept em in a golden birdcage
by the bed, guttling on cheese,

supping the claggy dregs
from the cocoa cup. I fed em crumbs
from mah lips, laid their collied yeds

on mah pillow as I slept
in a bone white nightdress, dreaming
o' fur, o' rough pink tongues.

eager sharp or cutting;   *wum* home;   *collied* blackened or sooty;
yeds heads

Fishwife

she brought oysters to my wedding
alive oh alive
laid out on a bridal bed of lemon and ice
slid her pearl-
handled knife between their tight lips
drew the stench of the sea

alive oh alive
I was seventeen and my groom forty-three
the crowd whooped as she linked our arms
and we swallowed   a gulp
of marriage   I gagged
on the salt   the slimy fecundity

I'd never known a man
and when we danced
my petticoats were foam on his thighs
alive oh alive
my mother wept for the rich times
my sisters waltzed around us
their bare arms swaying like a forest of kelp

as accordions wheezed
the Fishwife lifted my veil
and kissed me for luck   her lips O O
her tongue a plump trout
alive oh alive
men flipped silver in her skirts
sang of the tail she rubbed in brine in the tub
the gasping gills   raw beneath her blouse

when the night slithered dark
she watched with one milky eye
as he carried me up
the lamplight on the walls was tiny fleeing fish
alive oh alive   in the deepness I quivered
as he sliced me
from my bridal gown like a trawler-man's net
the bed was an ocean   I slipped
from my bare skin
alive oh alive   all tail   all fin
how the tide tossed
until alive ohhh alive
the wave flung my shining body   upon the rocks

Woodkeeper

Danger is delicious as the Candle Snuff and Sickener
you speak of in a hush. We're knee to knee on the moss-mattress,
the trees four-posters, your palm my plate,
your calloused fingers knife and fork. The blade is deft,
your touch gentlemanly on their white throats,
lifting the scarlet bonnets from their heads:
Bay Bollette, Freckled Flame Cap, Jew's Ear.

As we feast, love becomes a wood itself:
Enchanter's Nightshade, Wet-the-Beds, the shy ecstasy
of Ladies Smock in May. We roll on its floor, amongst beetles and ants,
your uniform soft as a shrew's snout, my body nothing but joy
and matter. When we cry, your voice is a tawny owl,
mine a pipistrelle battering the dusk.

And I am precious to you as a native tree: a hornbeam,
a beautiful sapling of a thing you fence off from children
with a special rope. You lie, all night, in my shivering roots,
tongue tracing the knots of my trunk until you bloom
from every cell. I will ripen you like a rare Chanterelle,
let you creep into tender cracks of my bark,
penetrate the dearest heartwood at my core.

Dog

You came back for me as a dog. Waited at my door
evening after evening that dark October, when even light
had lost its patience with our house. I knelt to you
in the yard, knew it was you by your eyes,
your mouth on my wrist, tender as on a whelp's neck.
I let you lick the perfume from my skin, lead me

from the house to the gap in the fence where the nettles
grew thick and downed as fur. *Come,* you urged,
and so I followed you through the streets, the common,
past the flats that lurched drunk above the ring road;
your nose to the wind, ears high in alert
as ambulances howled. There you laid me down

in the damp weeds below the railway line
where we'd once walked together and I cried
to feel your sides warm with content, your paw
in mine in the old way. *Let me stay*, I begged,
my mouth pressed to the velvet of your ear,
let the streets keep us in their den of dark.

But as your muzzle tipped my belly to the stars,
dogs how-wooed in the alleys around us, barked danger,
love-mourn, yelped at you to run, run, run;
and I knew that I would wake in the morning
with nothing left of you, my love, but your scent
on my skin, my clothes, my hair.

In the Steam Room

Here, any body
          might give you pleasure:
feet, shoulders, stomachs jewelled with veins
are sexless
          in the fug

which softens muscles to plasticine, slickens
freckled city skin,
                    liquefies flesh
until shapes shift,
          and we are all vapour

scorch-breathed and boundary-less,
filling the room
                    in white waves of perspiration,
our tongues nuzzling the neck
                    of the fat man
on the bench, easing
                    beneath the breasts
of the beautiful girl
          in the dripping blue swimsuit,

every pore an invitation,
                    every mouth, ear,
nostril, arsehole, rich anemoned seabed of cunt
a place for joy,

cells loosening and yielding in the heat,
          slackening

into pleasure
            deeper
                     then deeper
to that bodiless moment
                            when atoms met
and life gasped
          I'm coming, I'm coming
in the darkness.

Stone

When you bought me a milk pan for Christmas
a woman at work said you were *as romantic
as a stone*. Watching you that evening,
I wondered what stone she had meant –
a chip of car-park gravel or something fancier
like the peridot in my mother's engagement ring?

My interest in you became geological.
Pulling on your wellingtons to walk the dog in the rain,
you were granite, durable, funereal almost.
Under bath water, you were the agate
I found on Brighton beach as a child, sleek
and mottled as seal's skin.

At other times you seemed a rarer gem,
not emerald or topaz, nothing any other woman
would wear at her throat; but plainer, more lovely,
like the limestone walling caverns back home
that purified the iron in blast furnaces
where keepers dripped jet from their beading brows.

And a man like that would never choose a rose
or a diamond ring, he'd stand for hours in a shop
on the coldest day, testing the unfamiliar weight
of a pan in his hand, assessing its metal,
imagining how the milk would taste on my tongue
as it poured, steaming, from that perfect lip.

Bilston Enamels

Open me up
and peep at er inside,
Iris, head bowed in the factory
of er mom's back room, painting a throstle
wi' a brush med of a single black badger's hair.
Allus summat romantic: turtley doves, Portmeirion,
This and the giver are thine forever. Fancy tranklements
for folk to hold the relics of their lives: an auburn curl,
a babby's fust milk tooth like a Victorian sea pearl,
a gold ring, ticket stub, pinch of snuff, a folded
cutting from the Birmingham Post
about that lad who tumbled
like a pigeon from
the roof.

tranklements ornaments or trinkets; *fust* first

44

Darling Blue Eyes

July 7th
Dear Albert,
The night is so very starless now and I hold myself
perfectly still in the black,
coddled by the reist of my sisters,
their breath like wammels' breath, hot and mealy.
My dreams rile me and so I lie, eyes open,
your name on my tongue
until darkness creeps through my body like a robber
and thieves you from my mouth.
Darling. Where are you? No-one will tell me.
Your sweet E.

September 29th
Dear Love,
Your letters are faintling in my hope-box.
Darling blue eyes, they say, *darling   darling.*
I sing 'Lift Ye Voices' in the stifle of chapel
but I'm an empty vessel. Without you,
nothing is any good, not the day or the night,
not this black town where the bull drags
the only men left from their beds.
Everything is festering here: the slag heaps rise,
buds are brown, even my own name cankers
in my mouth like a crab apple. Eileen Gell.
Your Eileen Gell.

December 3rd
Dearest Bert,
Come back, my pet.

In my head, I wrap your face in soft cloth
and lover it away. Oh months, months of nothing.
Bring with you May, the rains, tipping rains,
when you held my little hand in Dimmocks Avenue
under the black eyes of the Ebenezer Baptist
darling   darling   you bowed your head to me,
the night air collied and soft as soot
and I said "help me, love, save me,
from I don't know what" for it was coming even then,
flooding over me like a great dark wave.
Your poor girl, your flower.

February 15th
My Albert,
Think of me, love, whatever camp may have you,
whosever bed may lull you, keep your head for me.
It's come over me again, that terrible rook.
In this house of women, this town of women,
my heart is clem-gutted.
Call me *darling* and hold out your hand to me
for I am a canary in a mine fluttering at the bars
as the darkness swoons me. Where are you, I beg?
Come back for me, I am losing myself. I am unpicking
myself like a sampler. I am so ashamed.
Darling   my darling. I sicken and fuss.

bull factory siren

46

Irene

It mizzled the night you died
but you'd already gone
back to your owd mon's garden
with your yellow frock on.
In the beds, goosegogs furred,
peas climbed cane wigwams,
your brothers' shirts danced
on the line. And you, thirteen
again, sensing light above,
raised your hand to shade
your eyes from the sun.

mizzled rained;   *owd mon* dad

The Sea of Talk

for dad

That last summer before school robbed language
from my mouth and parcelled it up in endless

Ladybird Books, you made me a boat of words
and pushed us off from the jetty into the Sea of Talk.

You let the waves navigate as my fingers stroked shoals
of nouns in the chatter – *goosegog, peony* –

verbs slithering, electric as eels in the seagrass.
All August we sailed, the vast shadows of stories

trawling below us: *'ow the lights waz out the night
you waz born... the secret in the marlpit up Batman's Hill...*

then further out, deeper, those first vowels we'd spoken,
filmy and shape-shifting as jellyfish in the dark.

You let me swim in the shallows until the moon drew
the murmuring tides to her breast; then you made a net

of your arms and hauled me in, kissed your thumb
to my small mouth, my ears, whispered:

*Bab, little wench, dow forget this place,
its babble never caught by ink or book*

*fer on land, school is singin' its siren song
and oysters clem their lips upon pearls in the muck...*

Miss Berry

I have learnt to write rows of o's bobbing
hopeful as hot air balloons from the line's tethers

and watched eight springs of frogspawn
grow legs but never...

and conducted clashy-bashy orchestras
of chime bars ocarina thundering tambour

and curled my hand over another hand
to hinge the crocodile jaws of the scissors.

I have accompanied a small mourning party
to a blackbird's burial plot

and rolled countless bodies, like coloured marbles,
across gym mats

and conducted science's great experiments
using darkened cupboards, plastic cups and cress

and unhooked a high window on a stuffy day
and heard the room's breath.

I have measured time by paper snowflakes,
blown eggs, bereft cocoons

and waved goodbye in summer so many times
that even in September my heart is June.

My Mother's Wedding Shoes

I try on your silver stilettos; ones you bought
before I was born, to wear at a wedding perhaps.

I can see you at nineteen, dancing
in the disco lights of the Working Men's Club,

your hair still long then, loose for the night.
Not knowing these shoes would send you dancing,

still a kid yourself, to that mithering bed of marriage;
six months later, you'd be stepping in them again

from the Mini's front seat to the registry office
a handful of flowers from the back garden

standing in for confetti, your mom crying
through her make-up, your bump not showing yet.

As a girl I longed to be fairytaled by shoes like these
while you kept me in lace-ups, classroom brogues

you'd polish each Sunday so your face shone back.
Now I understand what those plain soles meant:

Walk away, mah wench, from this town, that wedding.
Tek yer books an' yer sense an' keep on walking,

even if yo hear me blarting, dow ever turn back.

Goodnight Irene

Goodnight Irene, I say to you, goodnight,
as we follow the car to the cemetery, past the boarded
steelworks, the temple with its glittering dome,
the pubs no more than someone's front room
where faces sit like Toby Jugs in the bar lights;

over the canal bridge, the Baptist chapel
still brave on the cut, baptising the Sunday believers
in boat bilge, past the marlpit, the warehouses,
the Indian shop, the streets left to squatters,
their pebble-dashed terraces emptied by time.

We slow by the dog track, the red-iron gates
of the Jubilee Park, where metal horses run
to the railway and canter feral past city-bound trains.
Above us, your tower block sways in the wind
and the motorways loop like Cradley chain.

When you were a girl, these streets shone
like the coal, traipsing home with your dad from the pit's
black skeleton, your hand in his pocket, close as a kiss.
Now their names are music, a requiem:
Darkly Lane, Snow Hill, Roseville, Wren's Nest.

Wulfrun Hotel

Evenin's the best time fer waitin at the winder
fer someone yo love
as dusk is tossed like a magician's hanky
over the city's rooftops,
coverin secretaries beltin their macs as they nip
fer buses, men slippin
pink-eyed as rabbits from the black hat of the werks.

Then night, that owd conjuror,
gads in wi' 'is starry cape and fancy pigeons,
mekkin magic of the wenches
out chappin it on the cobbles, the lads touchin their lips
to the foam of the fust pint.

chappin it flirting or on the pull;   *fust* first

52

Echo

Hear me in abandoned bus shelters,
empty playgrounds
where bottles gather moss and cuckoo spit,
the corners of nightclubs,
clinics where bones push
at papery skin.

Wherever girls' voices are lost,
I am.

A gatherer of words –
buts, stops, whispered *no*s.
I scoop them in my fingers
like scattered pearls,
roll them on my tongue,
onto my song.

Wherever girls' voices are lost,
I am.

I had a voice once
until thirteen blew my speech
like the yolk from an egg,
left me hollow, pining
in the cave of my bedroom,
reed thin.

Wherever girls' voices are lost,
I am.

Now on brackened waste land
and screens where girls slip
from grainy footage
never seen again,
you will hear me singing

Wherever girls voices are lost,
I am.

Grasshopper Warbler

for Tom

Amongst the iris beds at Dimmingsdale
all May I waited,
sat out on the bow each evening
as day fell into the arms of night
and searched the twilight for your voice,
unpicking the dusk-song – for what?
A cricket, a mill wheel,
a girl spinning straw in her lonely tower?
I scanned the reedclumps and meadowsweet
for your skulking creep,
shy mouse-bird fossicking.

How those weeks seemed endless,
waiting too for the little creature that grew inside me
unseen, unheard, unknowable as you
in his private dark.
I was always listening, never unafraid.
I made fool's bargains with the fields:
keep jack-in-the-hedge flowering in an egg cup
and he would live;
see a kit – yes; four magpies – yes;
hear you, your song, your grasshopper song
to feel him trembling through me
like the wind through the reeds.

Nights I fretted you would never come,
the rushes alive with everything but you,
the moon waning too quickly into June.
I was heart-bare,

a shorn cornfield, willow stripped,
until that gloaming, sweet gloaming, weeks on,
when I heard you calling in the cut's half-light,
reeling and insistent as that tiny heartbeat.
Small bird, amongst the irises
I knelt and I wept.

The Way Home

Take me among the poplars
where beeches surrender to a path of gold;
before the silver birch,
its slender body tongued by the mouth of dusk.
Take my hand in yours as the path disappears
and do not turn from me
when I kneel to bury my old life in the wet earth,
the life I wept for those nights, the one I dreamt I would lose.

For our boy is waiting inside me,
his love a green bud, and nothing matters now but this,
this autumn afternoon in a singing copse
where we will lay ourselves down
like copper leaves,
that he may never step upon anything but light.

The Assumption

And we will go there again, make no mistake.
There will be no truants, no sly ghost-breaths
of smoke from behind the gates.
The air will be damp November, the fog lying soft
across the playing fields.

We will walk there without knowing,
heads down in the drizzle, fists stuffed in pockets
or holding the hand of a girl we used to love,
her laugh a mouthful of kali.
Our bodies will know the way.

And they will all be there, the ones we thought gone:
the moms, their mossy winter coats pulled close,
the sisters carting papier-mache projects of the galaxies
and the fathers, hands-scrubbed, who will bend
to gather up our shadows as we slip

through the buckle in the railings,
slender as we were, towards the cry
of a hand bell. And that smell, that smell
of clean pages, plasticine, the lavender
of Miss Dooley's throat as she bathes a graze.

Everything will be waiting: the pencils in pots,
a paper snowflake cast adrift from last year's blizzard
and, like a song rising up from the piano,
that daydream picture of Christ the Lamb,
beckoning the children into a field of white.

Christmas Eve

Tonight the Black Country is tinselled by sleet
falling on the little towns lit up in the darkness
like constellations – the Pigeon, the Collier –
and upon the shooting stars of boy racers
who comet through the streets in white Novas.
It's blowing in drifts from the pit banks,
over the brown ribbon of the cut, over Beacon Hill,
through the lap-loved chimneys of the factories.
Sleet is tumbling into the lap of the plastercast Mary
by the manger at St Jude's, her face gorgeous and naive
as the last Bilston carnival queen.
In the low-rise flats opposite the cemetery,
Mrs Showell is turning on her fibre-optic tree
and unfolding her ticket for the rollover lottery
though we ay never 'ad a bit o luck in ower lives
and upstairs in the box-rooms of a thousand semis
hearts are stuttering and minds unravelling
like unfinished knitting.
And the sleet fattens and softens to snow,
blanking the crowded rows of terraces
and their tiny hankies of garden, white now, surrendering
their birdfeeders and sandpits, the shed Mick built
last Autumn when the factory clammed up.
And the work's gone again
and the old boys are up at dawn to clock-on nowhere
except walk their dogs and sigh
at the cars streaming to call centres and supermarkets
because there ay nuthin in it that's mon's werk,
really bab, there ay...
But it's coming down now, really coming

over the stands at the Molineux, over Billy Wright
kicking his dreams into the ring road
and in the dark behind the mechanics
the O'Feeney's boy props his BMX against the lock-ups
and unzips to piss a flower into the snow
well gi' me strength, Lord, to turn the other cheek
fer we'm the only ones half way decent round ere
and the tower blocks are advent calendars,
every curtain pulled to reveal a snow-blurred face.
And it's Christmas soon, abide it or not,
for now the pubs are illuminated pink and gold
The Crooked House, Ma Pardoes, The Struggling Mon
and snow is filling women's hair like blossom
and someone is drunk already and throwing a punch
and someone is jamming a key in a changed lock
shouting *for christ's sake, Myra, yo'll freeze me to jeth*
and a hundred new bikes are being wrapped in sheets
and small pyjamas warmed on fireguards
and children are saying *one more minute, just one, Mom*
and the old girls are watching someone die on a soap
and feeling every snow they've ever seen set in their bones.
It's snowing on us all
and I think of you, Eloise, down there in your terrace,
feeding your baby or touching his hand to the snow
and although we can't ever go back or be what we were
I can tell you, honestly, I'd give up everything I've worked for
or thought I wanted in this life,
to be with you tonight.

The Night You Were Born

It was a month before me, all the lights
in the Black Country out for the evening,

Wrens Nest tucked under a blanket of darkness,
mithered only by the fog-beams of your dad's van

as it sped to the hospital. In the back, the dog,
snuffling in her bed of tools and wood shavings.

In the front, your mom, panting on the turns,
her frightened moon face waning at the window.

I think about that night when I doze, heavy
with our son, in the snow-soft hours.

What it would have been to have seen you, pushed
howling, from that red tent of legs,

the first word on the page of our story.
I press myself against you in the darkness, listen

for your murmur as he moves inside me. Oh love,
I can almost hear it now: that first cry –

a raw thread of sound spooling through winter
to stitch our lives together.

Notes & Acknowledgements

'Bilston Enamels' were little enamelled decorative boxes made in Bilston in the Black Country, often painted at home by women pieceworkers.

'Darling Blue Eyes' was written using extracts from my grandparents' wartime letters.

Acknowledgements are due to the editors of the following publications in which some of these poems first appeared: *Ambit, Artemis, Brittle Star, Days of Roses, Magma, Mslexia, The North, Poetry London, Poetry News, Poetry Review, Poetry Wales, The Rialto, Silk Road Review, Smiths Knoll, Under the Radar.* 'Birmingham Roller' was commended in the National Poetry Competition 2011; 'Bird' and 'Sow' received first and second prize in the Poetry London Competition in 2011 and 2012. 'The Black Delph Bride' and 'Gosty Hill' were commissioned by The Poetry Society and The Canal and River Trust for the *Waterlines* Project in 2013. Some of these poems were published in the pamphlet *The Patron Saint of Schoolgirls,* Tall Lighthouse, 2010. A selection of these poems has also been recorded for the Poetry Archive.

I'm grateful to The Society of Authors for an Eric Gregory Award, and to Arvon and The Jerwood Foundation for their invaluable support and mentoring. Thanks to Jo and Andrew at Royal Holloway, to my brilliant workshop groups for their feedback and friendship, to Declan, to Parisa and all at Chatto, and to my wonderful mentor Daljit.

Love and thanks to my family, especially James without whom this book could never have been written.